Earthquakes and Man

Of the countless earthquakes that happen each year, the vast majority are not large enough to be felt, and their existence is known only to *seismologists* who study the evidence obtained from sensitive recording instruments. A few earthquakes each year make world headlines but these are not necessarily the largest. An earthquake will bring great death and destruction only if it is violent enough to cause damaging shaking in a densely populated region where buildings are not constructed to withstand earthquakes; even then few lives may be lost unless the earthquake strikes when most people are indoors. Moreover, as cities grow and become more sophisticated, the potential for financial disaster increases enormously. For example, the 1980 El Asnam earthquake in Algeria was a disaster in both financial and human terms. Although it was not of great magnitude, its origin was near a city built on poor ground. The earthquake occurred during peak shopping hours when thousands were in the new shopping centre, which collapsed on them. Modern blocks of flats built on piers became uninhabitable when the piers gave way: in all 300 000 people were made homeless and 2500 died.

In historical records, earthquakes are commonly ascribed to the location where most damage and human suffering occurred—that is, the nearest important centre of habitation. But the earthquake may in reality have originated tens of kilometres away in remote territory where there was no-one to feel it and no building to be destroyed. For example, records suggest Antioch to be a highly seismic place, but many of the earthquakes which caused damage in the city may have been far more intense in the surrounding countryside. When building up a history in order to forecast the likely size, distribution and frequency of earthquakes, it is important to understand why a particular earthquake brings about a disaster, so that historical records are interpreted correctly, in order to avoid misleading conclusions such as that cities are more earthquake-prone than rural regions. The historical record is patchy and it is not easy to put together a long record which is consistent in quality. Sometimes evidence comes from unexpected sources. The bas-relief in fig 2 from the house of L. C. Jucundus in Pompeii depicts an earthquake of AD 63 in which the Capitolium, flanked by equestrian statues, is collapsing. The temples at Luxor (fig 4) were damaged by an earthquake which took place during Roman times, probably 27 BC. The temple at the Agora, Athens, now known as the temple of Hephaistos, is contemporary with the Parthenon, similar in style but smaller. Earthquake damage is seen on its southern aspect where the column blocks are displaced (fig 5), but not sufficiently to cause collapse. The method of construction of these columns, where the blocks are tied by a lead pin, may even be an early example of earthquake-resistant building. Whilst many buildings must have been destroyed in antiquity by earthquakes, their better-built neighbours survive, and their continuing existence should not

2 Roman bas-relief depicting a contemporary earthquake

3 The eroded remains of a village wall, Iran, earthquake-damaged in 1923

4 Earthquake damage at Luxor

5 Earthquake damage at Athens

be taken as an indication of lack of earthquakes. Sometimes evidence of earthquake damage is obliterated rapidly, not only by demolition and the re-use of building materials, but also by natural erosion processes. Fig 3 shows the remains of the adobe walls of a fortified village settlement in Iran, damaged by an earthquake in 1923. The village was rebuilt nearby, and the remains of the abandoned settlement are now barely recognisable. In general, earthquakes occur in zones related to the large-scale geological structure of the Earth (fig 6). The Bible mentions earthquakes a number of times, and those associated with the Dead Sea rift system are shown in the figure. Evidently earthquakes were then sufficiently infrequent to have been used as time-references; thus the earthquake referred to in the book of Amos is the same one as that in Zechariah. The Dead Sea system appears to have even fewer earthquakes now than in the past, but this is probably a temporary respite. The Anatolian fault zone was particularly active between AD 100 and 500 and from AD 1000 to the present day, and the converse is shown by the Border zone. Thus it seems that, whilst locally there may be variations in numbers and severity of earthquakes, on a global scale there is no clear indication that earthquake activity is on the increase or decrease.

I. SAMUEL 14

15 And there was trembling in the host, in the field, and among all the people: the garrison, and the spoilers, they also trembled, and the earth quaked: so it was a very great trembling.
16 And the watchmen of Saul in Gib′-ė-åh of ... and, behold, t ... ed away, and ... ing down one ...

ST. MATTHEW 27

51 And, behold, the veil of the temple was rent in twain from the top to the bottom; and the earth did quake, and the rocks rent;

AMOS 1

THE words of Amos, who was among the herdmen of Tė-ko′-à, which he saw concerning Israel in the days of Ŭz-zi′-àh king of Judah, and in the days of Jėr-ò-bo′-àm the son of Jo′-àsh king of Israel, two years before the earthquake.
2 And he said, THE LORD will roar from Zi ... voice from J ... habitations of ... mourn, and ... shall wither. ...

ZECHARIAH 14

5 And ye shall flee to the valley of the mountains; for the valley of the mountains shall reach unto Ā′-żl: yea, ye shall flee, like as ye fled from before the earthquake in the days of Ŭz-zi′-àh king of Judah: and the LORD my God shall come, and all the saints with thee.

6 The locations of some Biblical earthquakes in the Dead Sea rift system, and their relation to other earthquake zones

Living through an earthquake

The events of an earthquake can be pieced together from independent lines of evidence. First, instruments may have been suitably placed to record ground movement, and secondly, study of the damage yields invaluable clues. Eyewitness accounts augment these, even though it may not be easy to reconcile different reports of the same event. At most, shaking lasts a few minutes, but if it is violent, those present will be shocked by the experience even if they are uninjured; in such circumstances calm observation is not easy. The following descriptions and artists' reconstructions illustrate some of the largest earthquakes of all time.

In the Assam district of India in 1897 Mr A. E. Shuttleworth at first attributed the trembling of his bungalow to thunder, but as the shaking increased, he realised it was an earthquake: 'as the timbers all began to crack and the verandah floor to split under our feet I hurried my wife outside into the rain, which was coming down in torrents. It was as much as I could do to hold my wife up. We then saw the earth all round heaving in a most frightful manner. The earth resembled waves coming from opposite directions and meeting in a great heap and then falling back; each time the waves seemed to fall back the ground opened slightly, and each time they met, water and sand were thrown up to a height of about 18 inches or so. The shock was strong enough to knock over a couple of elephants I had in camp with me . . . On re-entering the bungalow . . . we could not shut any of the doors that were opened nor open the doors that were shut.'

The Lisbon earthquake of 1755 struck on the morning of November 1st, All Saints' Day; Richard Wolsall, a British surgeon, wrote to James Parsons, a colleague in London, 'and then came down every church and convent in town, together with the King's palace, the magnificent opera-house, joining to it; in short, there was not a large building in town that escaped. It far exceeds all description, for the fear and consternation was so great, that the most resolute person durst not stay a moment to remove a few stones off the friend he loved most, though many might have been saved by so doing: but nothing was thought of but self-preservation; getting into open places, and into the middle of streets, was the most probable security. Such, as were in the upper stories of houses, were in general more fortunate than those, that attempted to escape by the doors; for they were buried under the ruins with the greatest part of the foot-passengers: such as were in equipages escaped best, though their cattle and drivers suffered severely; but those lost in houses and the streets are very unequal in number to those, that were buried in the ruins of churches; for as it was a day of great devotion, and the time of celebrating mass, all the churches in the city were vastly crouded.'

The Great Alaska earthquake of 1964 caused intense shaking at Seward. 'Dean Smith was about 50 ft above the Alaska Railroad dock, working in the operator's cabin in the gantry crane on berth No.1. As the shaking got worse, the top of the crane flipped back and forth "like a long whip". The wheels came clear of the tracks and the entire crane was "walking around like some stiff-legged spider". By the time he scrambled down, there were cracks in the paving of the dock that were a foot wide and "getting bigger all the time".'

Seward harbour fell into the sea along with part of the Alaska Railroad terminus, in a submarine landslide, thus wiping out the livelihood of the town, which was based on shipping. Edmund Endresen escaped from the harbour area, running over ground that was 'like walking on a rubber mattress'. 'At the railroad tracks, box-cars that stood between Edmund Endresen and high ground were rocking violently from side to side. Attempting to cross the tracks by crawling under one of them, he fell into a crack 3 ft wide and about 30–40 ft deep, adjacent to the west track. He clung to the side of the opening which, as it began to close, filled with water, floating

him to the top. He was nearly clear when the crack closed on one of his feet, which he wrenched violently to get free. As he got to his feet, the boxcar he had just crawled under was disappearing and he had only a glimpse of it before it sank from sight, He ran a few more feet and jumped another crack about 3 ft wide. Numerous cracks about 12–18 in. wide appeared in the next 500 ft from the shoreline, but by the time he reached Fourth Avenue, there were no more cracks opening in the ground and Edmund stopped to catch his breath.'

Tsunamis, and water waves generated by a landslide damaged Seward. Tom Hyde saw out on the bay a 'series of gigantic waves with glassy smooth but curling fronts hurling towards the shore with breakneck speed'. After the shaking was over, Gilbert O Nelson was driving towards the town. He 'stopped at the end of the main runway and saw a muddy wave in the bay directly to the south and traveling northwestward. The wave was rolling, not breaking, and sounded like a fast freight train. Boats, trees, and other debris were carried on its crest. Nelson turned the car around and drove up the old landing strip, traveling about 70 mph with the wave coming up the strip right behind him. He said there appeared to be a great rush of wind immediately preceding the wall of water. The wave toppled the old Civil Air Patrol house near the southeast end of the runway and carried it up the field. The wave almost reached the cross-strip of the runway, about ¼ mi from the beach. Nelson's motor failed and the rest of his family fled on foot to the end of the runway.'

Quotations from *The Great Alaska Earthquake of 1964, Summary and Recommendations,* by permission of the National Academy of Sciences, Washington, DC.

Valdez dock was broken up by the shaking even before it disappeared, with the rest of the waterfront, into the turbulent water created by the submarine slide (p 13). Captain M. D. Stewart, aboard the SS *Chena* which was unloading freight at the dock, ran to the bridge when the shaking started: 'The Valdez piers started to collapse right away. There was a tremendous noise. The ship was laying over to port. I had been in earthquakes before, but I knew right away that this was the worst one yet. The *Chena* raised about 30 feet on an oncoming wave. The whole ship lifted and heeled to port about 50°. Then it was slammed down heavily on the spot where the docks had disintegrated moments before. I saw people running – with no place to run to. It was just ghastly. They were just engulfed by buildings, water, mud and everything. The *Chena* dropped where the people had been. That is what has kept me awake for days . . . I could see the land (at Valdez) jumping and leaping in a terrible turmoil. We were inside of where the dock had been. We had been washed into where the small boat harbour used to be. There was no water under the *Chena* for a brief interval. I realized we had to get out quickly if we were ever going to get out at all.' The *Chena* 'steamed away from shore, scraping bottom several times and wallowing around . . .

In Valdez town, about 70 km from the epicentre, the shaking was violent and accompanied by a continuous roar. Charles H. Clark, a geologist with the Alaska Department of Highways, observed: 'The first tremors were hard enough to stop a moving person, and shock waves were immediately noticeable on the surface of the ground . . . After about one minute, the amplitude or strength of the shock waves increased in intensity and failures in buildings as well as the frozen ground surface began to occur. Cracks in the roadway surface opened and closed again as the troughs and crests passed the failure. These cracks opened as much as 3 feet, but the most frequent failures were only opened several inches. As these cracks closed due to passing of a shock wave trough, water from both ground-water sources and broken sewers and water pipes squirted in a spray about 20 feet into the air . . . The amplitude of the waves was estimated by observance of my son standing about 410 feet away. He is 6 feet tall and was in plain sight during most of the earthquake. As a crest passed him, he would appear in full sight with one depression between himself and me. As he entered a trough, he would appear to sink out of sight up to about 1 foot below belt line. This would indicate that he rose and fell about three to four feet.'

Anchorage was damaged by landslides, and by shaking which completely demolished some larger buildings. Connie Casey ran out of the Westward Hotel as the shaking began: 'All the ground was weaving like an ocean wave. It really seemed like trying to balance yourself on a ball. We could see pavement breaks. All the glass was out of the Northern Commercial Building. There was debris all over. We looked down Fifth Avenue and could not believe the crazy angle of the J. C. Penney Store. It was almost like we were in a daze, and couldn't believe the things we saw. . . . We got home and changed into warm clothing, not even realizing we were wet from falling and sitting in the snow.'

Running out of a nearby bar, Bert Londerville saw cars rolling back and forth, 'with cracks opening all around. I happened to be looking toward the Anchorage Hardware store when it fell. Then the building adjoining the Hofbrau started falling, and I could hear the kitchen and bar of the Hofbrau falling, although the back wall stood up. The next thing I can remember is looking toward the Westward Hotel, seeing it sway, and wondering what kept it from falling down. I will probably always remember the screams of the people on the top floors of the hotel. It seemed as though the ground was moving in all directions – sideways, in circles, and up and down.'

A landslide at Turnagain Heights, an attractive residential quarter of Anchorage, carried whole houses seawards (fig 7). Robert Atwood was at home and 'In a few short moments it was obvious that this earthquake was no minor one: the chandelier made from a ship's wheel swayed too much. Things were falling that had never fallen before. I headed for the door. At the door I saw walls weaving. On the driveway I turned and watched my house squirm and groan. Tall trees were falling in our yard. I moved to a spot where I thought it would be safe, but, as I moved, I saw cracks appear in the earth. Pieces of ground in jigsaw-puzzle shapes moved up and down, tilted at all angles. I tried to move away, but more appeared in every direction. I noticed that my house was moving away from me, fast. As I started to climb the fence to my neighbor's yard, the fence disappeared. Trees were falling in crazy patterns. Deep chasms opened up. Table-top pieces of earth moved upward, standing like toadstools with great overhangs, some were turned at crazy angles. A chasm opened beneath me. I tumbled down. I was quickly on the verge of being buried. I ducked pieces of trees, fence posts, mailboxes, and other odds and ends. Then my neighbor's house collapsed and slid into the chasm. For a time it threatened to come down on top of me, but the earth was still moving, and the chasm opened to receive the house. When the earth movement stopped, I climbed on the top of the chasm. I found angular landscape in every direction. I found my neighbor carrying his young daughter. We found his wife atop one of the high mushroom-like promontories. She was standing alone with her auto, marooned. We climbed up and down chasm walls and under dangerous overhanging pieces of frozen ground to safety.'

From *The Prince William Sound, Alaska, earthquake of 1964 and aftershocks,* permission NOAA.

H. BOLTON SEED

7 Turnagain Heights landslide, caused by liquefaction of subsurface sediment in the prolonged shaking

Earthquake damage

The huge toll of human life taken by earthquakes is largely attributable to failure of homes to withstand ground shaking. Building methods and styles are generally dictated by the local climate, the types of construction material available nearby, and by fashion and tradition. Even in many of the world's most seismic regions, earthquake-resistant construction is not always the first consideration. In arid and semi-arid regions all over the world, sunbaked clay brick — adobe — has been the traditional construction material for thousands of years. It is cheap, easily worked, readily available where other materials are scarce, and provides a cool, equable interior. But adobe buildings have a low resistance to earthquake shaking. In parts of Iran, villages are expanded by attaching new adobe units to existing ones, so that an entire group of houses is dependent on the oldest unit in the centre. Further, the domed roofs are thick and heavy. In 1968 an earthquake badly damaged or totally destroyed adobe buildings (fig 8), leaving tens of thousands homeless, whilst the few better-made structures were relatively unharmed. This was probably the most damaging shock in the area for 800 years; fortunately it occurred during the afternoon, when many people were in the fields and thus escaped being entombed in their homes. Earthquake damage is cumulative, so that the longer shaking continues, the greater is the damage. Most earthquakes last less than a minute, but an exceptionally long one might last four or more minutes. A series of short earthquakes could produce the same amount of damage as one long earthquake. Western Sicily was struck by a series of earthquakes in 1968, none of which was particularly large (maximum magnitude 6), but

8 Village in Khorasan province, Iran, devastated in 1968

9 Venzone Cathedral, Italy (left) after main shock (right) after aftershocks

cumulatively the damage to the old masonry buildings was severe, rendering some towns totally uninhabitable (fig 1). Buildings which have been weakened by a major shock may not appear too badly damaged (fig 9), but in the smaller *aftershocks* which invariably plague an earthquake area for several months, much greater damage may result. It is difficult to rescue survivors trapped under fallen masonry when at any moment an aftershock may cause further collapse of weakened buildings, burying the rescuers too. For this reason alone, it can be weeks or months before reliable estimates of the earthquake toll are available. In general, unreinforced masonry buildings, especially if they are old, fare very badly in earthquakes. Furthermore, many people have been killed by collapse of chimneys, parapets, balconies and decorative stonework in the rush to get out of doors when shaking starts. The damage to a baroque church in Antigua (fig 11) shows how utterly inappropriate this style is for earthquake regions. Multi-storey buildings are not necessarily hazardous provided they are adequately designed and built, but failure to tie walls to floors results in collapse like a playing-card house (fig 10).

The destruction in San Francisco caused by the 1906 earthquake — panorama below — showed that buildings on made ground, alluvium and water-soaked sediments suffer greater damage than those founded on solid rock. Adequately sited wooden houses survived the shaking, only to be consumed in the fire (p 35). The few steel-framed buildings then in existence performed well: none was so badly damaged as to be unsafe.

The place on the earth's surface directly above the *initial* point of the rupture which generates an earthquake is the *epicentre*, and in small earthquakes, damage decreases with distance from the epicentre. This simple relation does not hold for large earthquakes where the rock may be ruptured for hundreds of kilometres, and places close to the rupture suffer intense damage, although far from the epicentre. Damage also depends upon the radiation pattern of the seismic waves emitted and their frequency spectrum: the 1964 Alaska earthquake produced large quantities of low-frequency vibration to which the small-scale buildings in Alaska were not sensitive. Had there existed bigger structures to resonate with these frequencies, damage would have been more severe.

10 Collapsed multi-storey building, Nicaragua

11 Damaged church in Antigua, Guatemala

Whilst lives are lost in earthquakes when dwellings collapse, other man-made structures fail and cause further havoc. Communications may be interrupted by damage to roads, railways, bridges, telephone systems, radio and TV stations, and airports. Failure of dams and destruction of factories involved with dangerous chemicals kill people and harm the environment. Damage to emergency services, hospitals, fire stations and electricity, gas and water supplies (fig 12) helps the spread of fire and disease in the chaotic aftershock-filled days.

Railways and roads are likely to be blocked by landslides: the rail tracks may be deformed and road surfaces thrown into a jumble of confused blocks separated by gaping fissures. Road and rail bridges and overpass systems are vulnerable, the damage necessitating detours which delay traffic at a time when rapid movement of supplies and people could mean the difference between life and death. The San Fernando, California, earthquake of 1971 was of only moderate magnitude (6.4) but because it was shallow (13km) it caused heavy shaking, greater than building codes had anticipated, so that over a small area significant damage occurred. Overpasses in the state freeway system were damaged (fig 13) where supporting columns failed due to inadequate reinforcement or to rotation of bridge spans which had a large skew. Highways on embankments were damaged by settlement of the fill material, and cut slopes produced landslides. County roads and bridges were also damaged but within

four days all were negotiable with caution. Damage at generating stations and to transmission lines interrupted electricity supplies, but service was mostly restored after two days. Gas pipes were damaged, but were quickly isolated with minimum disruption to supplies and very little outbreak of fire. Water and sewerage facilities were extensively damaged because the epicentre was close to the complex of reservoirs, pumping stations and treatment plants that supplied most of Los Angeles city water. Dams retaining two reservoirs, the Upper and Lower Van Norman dams, were both damaged. A substantial part of the lower dam slid into the lake (fig14) but fortunately the water level was low at the time and no water slopped over. As it was thought the dam might fail in aftershocks, 80 000 people were evacuated from the area downstream until the lake was drained to a safer level. No water escaped through the damaged upper dam, which was fortunate as the weakened lower dam could not have withstood the extra water load. Several hospitals in the region of most intensive shaking suffered badly (fig 15). Like the dams, the hospitals complied with local building codes, but it is important to realise that these specify *minimum* requirements. Therefore buildings which only just meet code requirements can be regarded as only marginally safe. It is important that hospitals, in particular, are designed and built to the highest standards, not only because they should present no hazard to life and limb, but also because they must

12 Water escaping from a broken main in Anchorage, Alaska

13 Damaged freeway interchange near San Fernando, California

continue to provide an essential service to the victims of the earthquake; they also, of course, represent a high capital investment. Besides hospitals and dams there are other structures that should be built to high earthquake-resistive standards, including for example, nuclear power stations and factories dealing with explosive or toxic substances. A liquid petroleum gas plant in California, built to an earthquake-resistive specification, suffered little direct damage in the Kern County earthquake of 1952, but five butane gas storage vessels in the same plant were not constructed to the same standard. Two collapsed in the shaking, allowing escape of the heavier-than-air gas, which ignited and set fire to the whole plant (fig 16). In urban areas, fire succeeding an earthquake is a very real hazard and efforts should be made to protect the water system from breakdown; all buildings designed to resist shaking should also be fire-resistive. An interesting example of an earthquake- and fire-resistive building was the Imperial Hotel in Tokyo designed by Frank Lloyd Wright. Built between 1916 and 1922 on an inauspicious site (filled ground on watery mud), the structure, with suitable foundations, was kept light-weight by use of porous lava and thin brick facings, and copper roof tiles, with flexible plumbing and wiring and a large ornamental pool. In 1923 Tokyo was razed by an earthquake and consequent fire but the hotel survived virtually unharmed, water from the pool being used to keep the conflagration at bay when the city water supply failed.

15 Collapsed ground floor and wing of Olive View Hospital, California

14 Landslide of embankment dam near San Fernando, California

16 Fire following earthquake at LPG plant, Paloma, California

Reducing earthquake risk

One way to reduce vulnerability to earthquakes is by predicting their onset and evacuating inhabitants at risk (p 32). Alternatively, buildings can be sited, designed and built so that in an earthquake they are not dangerous and the cost of repairs is reduced. To do this the *seismic hazards,* that is such earthquake effects as surface rupturing, ground shaking, ground liquefaction, landsliding and flooding, must first be evaluated (fig 17). *Surface rupturing* should be considered likely in future earthquakes at any *fault* (break in the rock, p 20) where there has been geologically recent movement. *Ground shaking* is most intense near the rupturing fault, decreasing with distance, but the local geology affects the intensity, for example soft sediments amplify shaking. Soft sediments are also liable to *liquefaction* – they become quicksand – depending on the nature of the sediment particles, their density of packing and content of pore water, coupled with the intensity and duration of shaking. Heavy objects may founder (fig 18) or buried light objects such as septic tanks rise to the surface, and fountains of muddy or sandy water are sometimes ejected (p 6) even after shaking ceases. *Landslides* (see also p 29) are a hazard, particularly in hilly or mountainous regions, after heavy rain and where slopes are already unstable because of rock type or sparse vegetation. *Flooding* from tsunamis (p 14) is a hazard in coastal districts; it may

also result from ground level changes, from ponding up of rivers by earthquake-induced landslides (p 29), or failure of dams. After hazards have been identified, a hypothetical earthquake, called the *design earthquake,* is selected for this area, based on the largest earthquake thought possible on the longest active fault in the region and its likely frequency of occurrence. This is problematical as data are always inadequate; for example, selection of too small a design earthquake contributed to the damage caused by the San Fernando earthquake (p 10–11). Seismic hazard zone maps can then be drawn up for land-use planning and building codes established. In practice, however, it is not easy to achieve a good match between land use and seismic risk, especially in established settlements, where moving existing structures to less hazardous locations may well be considered prohibitively expensive. After a devastating earthquake, the benefit of rebuilding an entire city at a different site, in the hope of avoiding future damage, may be considered. For example, the city of Scupi in Yugoslavia, after damage in AD 518, was rebuilt as Skopje, a few kilometres away. The new site proved no better, as the earthquake in 1963 demonstrated. A subsequent investigation showed that there was no less hazardous site in the vicinity, so rebuilding incorporated many earthquake-resistive features.

ground shaking decreasing in intensity with distance from the fault

liquefaction of recent sediments

landslides in hilly ground

amplification of low frequency ground shaking

surface ruptures

flooding in low lying coastal regions

fault

bedrock

recent sediments

17 Earthquake hazards related to topography and geological structure

H BOLTON SEED

18 Undamaged blocks of flats foundered into liquefied ground, Japan, 1964

The town of Valdez in Alaska was severely hit by the 1964 earthquake. Ground shaking was amplified by the soft sediments of the delta on which Valdez stood; and the extent of the ground movement was estimated by an eye witness (p 6). The fountains of water he describes suggest that liquefaction also occurred. A submarine landslide of the seaward end of the delta carried away the harbour region (fig 20) and raised water waves which swept into the town, causing further damage. Afterwards it was decided to relocate Valdez in a safer site, and Mineral Creek, only a few kilometres away, was chosen (fig 20). Now situated on an alluvial fan of coarse cobbles, well drained and protected on the seaward side by a buttress of bedrock, Valdez has been laid out and built incorporating earthquake-resistive features. Valdez was selected as the year-round ice-free port on mainland Alaska for the terminal of the Trans-Alaska oil pipeline. The line crosses rugged permafrost terrain, animal migration routes and active faults in a seismic region, but incorporates features to protect both the massive capital investment in the pipeline itself and all aspects of the environment through which it passes. Its zig-zag path, the Teflon-coated low-friction supports and the wide spacing of the anchor points allow flexing during ground shaking, and closely spaced cut-off valves permit control of oil spillage should a break occur. The terminal near Valdez is built on solid bedrock and most facilities are high enough to avoid damage by tsunamis.

19 (above) **The trans-Alaska oil pipeline** transports crude oil from the fields in Northern Alaska more than 1000 km to the deepwater terminal at Jackson Point near Valdez, whence tankers transfer the oil to refineries in the western USA.

20 (below) **Valdez was resited** after the disastrous 1964 earthquake when a technical study showed a much safer site nearby. Every effort has been made to ensure that these installations are earthquake-resistant, but where the design earthquake is so large, it is impossible to say they are totally earthquake-proof.

outwash delta

Valdez old site

Trans-Alaska oil pipeline

Jackson Point

alluvial fan

Mineral Creek new site

submarine slump

bedrock

'Tidal waves'

Seismic sea waves, known as *tsunamis* (and popularly as *'tidal waves'*), are induced by a sudden large vertical movement of the sea bed caused by a submarine volcanic explosion or a major earthquake. The disturbance of the water travels outwards as a series of waves, at speeds which depend on the water depth along their path. The waves are imperceptible in mid-ocean, but near coastlines they increase in height as they are slowed down by the shallowing water, and in some places can approach the shore as towering walls of water many metres high. They have sometimes been responsible for more deaths than the rest of the phenomena associated with the earthquake or eruption.

Almost all tsunamis occur in the Pacific Ocean, and subsequent to a disastrous tsunami in 1946 a warning system centred on Honolulu Observatory was set up for the entire Pacific Ocean. Based on a number of contributing tide stations and seismic observatories around the Pacific, the system incorporates tsunami detectors and seismic recording apparatus which trigger an alarm immediately a likely event is recorded. These observations are sent to Honolulu Observatory which is responsible for issuing warnings if necessary. Eight minutes after the beginning of the great Alaska earthquake in 1964, arrival of the first seismic waves at Honolulu triggered the alarm (fig 21). Information from seismic observatories in Alaska had not at that time arrived at Honolulu because the control tower at Anchorage International Airport which usually transmitted their communications had been destroyed. It was not until reports arrived from more distant seismic observatories that the epicentre and magnitude of the earthquake could be determined, and an earthquake advisory bulletin was then issued, an hour and a half after the shock began. The first sighting of a tsunami was at Kodiak, and after this report was received at Honolulu, a tsunami-warning bulletin was issued, by which time the first sea wave was approaching the Canadian coast, approximately the limit of perceptible shaking. A snag in the system is the inherent delays which mean warnings are too late for the epicentral region of a quake. But those living near the Pacific coast know from experience when they feel the shaking that a tsunami may follow. Because tsunamis travel at a speed which varies only with water depth it is possible to predict the expected arrival time anywhere in the Pacific once the epicentre is located.

21 Approximate locations of the first wave of the tsunami at hourly intervals after the 1964 Alaska earthquake

Alaska Coastal regions were inundated by tsunamis. Travelling in the shallow waters on the continental shelf, the first wave took an hour to reach Kodiak, by which time most of the population had been evacuated. With great difficulty Kodiak Naval Station managed to inform Honolulu Observatory of the tsunamis.

Port Alberni The first wave put the tide gauge out of action. The second and third waves, estimated to have been 9 metres high, were amplified by the narrow fiord.

Crescent City bay invariably amplifies tsunamis, whatever their direction of approach. Those drowned had not expected the big third and fourth waves and had returned prematurely to clean up.

San Francisco Although a warning had been received, and attempts made to evacuate coastal areas, newspapers estimated that ten thousand people crowded to the beach areas to watch the waves arrive. Fortunately the waves were only 2 metres high here.

Port Alberni

Crescent City

San Francisco

Area of uplift and subsidence in which tsunami was generated.

Kodiak

Honolulu Observatory issued a warning to all participants in the Tsunami Warning System about three hours after the earthquake, that a severe earthquake in Alaska had generated a sea wave whose arrival in Hawaii was expected 2½ hours later.

Seiches are water waves induced in lakes, ponds and reservoirs by large earthquakes, at considerable distances from the source of the earthquake, and result from disturbances caused by seismic surface waves (p 20). Nearer to large earthquakes, oscillations of water could be of quite different origin; they may be brought about by landslides falling into water, causing the water to slop back and forth, or may be the result of tsunamis. It may therefore be difficult to unravel the causes of the various water waves associated with large coastal earthquakes. The Lisbon earthquake of 1 November 1755, which happened at half past nine in the morning, generated seiches over much of Europe (fig 22). At Portsmouth at 10 o'clock HMS *Gosport*, a 40-gun ship, pitched backwards and forwards with the water in her dock. Canals, moats and millponds as well as lakes and rivers in Britain were disturbed, in places leaving fish on dry land, and startling man and beast alike (fig 23). Spa waters near Prague unprecedentedly ran muddy and changed their flow rate between eleven in the morning and twelve noon. Even making allowances for inaccuracies of time-keeping, which may have been considerable, the seiches are distinguishable from later tsunamis which were reported as arriving in the afternoon in extreme south-west England and early evening in the Bristol Channel, having been greatly slowed by the shallow waters of the continental shelf. The Alaska earthquake of 1964 caused seiches over most of North America – in Oregon about 10 minutes after the quake began, and some 20 minutes later in Florida. Evidence from this 1964 earthquake indicates that geological structure influences seiching: the Mexican Gulf region showed a high concentration of seiches, probably because of amplification of surface waves in thick sediments there, whilst the Appalachian Mountains apparently absorbed the waves, as few seiches were recorded south-east of the range.

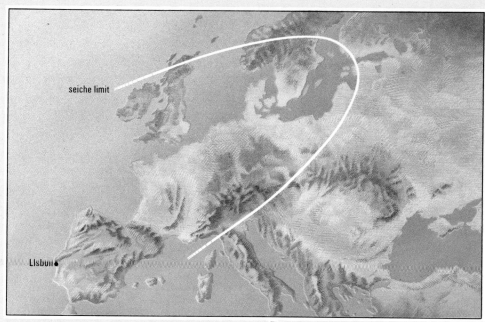

seiche limit

Lisbon

22 Seiches from Lisbon earthquake, 1755 . . .

23 . . . were observed in England

From Swithin Adee, *M. D. F. R. S. to* Philip Carteret Webb, *Esq; F. R. S.*

Read Nov. 27, 1755.

SIR,   Guildford, Nov 25, 1755.

I Have met with a very particular account of the agitation of the water on the 1st of this month. An old sensible serious man, at Mrs. Wilson's, in the parish of Cobham, was watering a horse in hand, at a pond close by the house, which is fed by springs, and had no current. The time he fixes was about ten in the morning, but their clock goes too flow. While the horse was drinking, the water run away from the horse, and moved towards the south with swiftness, and in such a quantity, as left the bottom of the pond bare, then returned with that impetuosity, which made the man leap backwards, to secure himself from the sudden approach of the water. It went back again to the south, with a great swell, and returned again. Upon inspecting the place, I found the water must have risen above one foot. The ducks were alarmed at the first agitation, and flew all instantly out of the pond. The man observed, that there was a particular calm at this time of day. You will observe here were two fluxes and two refluxes seen distinctly. This phænomenon will not be very surprising, since we have heard of the earthquake in Spain and Portugal. I am,

SIR, S. Adee.

Studying earthquakes

The earliest known instrument for detecting earthquakes was invented in AD 132 by the Chinese philosopher Zhang Heng. This sizable instrument, some two metres in diameter and made of bronze, has apparently not survived, but is known from contemporary descriptions. The model in fig 25 is a modern reconstruction from these descriptions. The inferred mechanism of the apparatus, whereby relative movement of the massive central pendulum causes a dragon's mouth to open, releasing a ball which drops into the mouth of an attendant toad, is illustrated in fig 26. Direction was given by which of the eight dragon heads had moved, but constant observation was necessary to determine the arrival time of the shock waves. Apparently the apparatus was sufficiently sensitive to detect imperceptible shaking, as it registered an earthquake over 600 km away, news of which only arrived days later by messenger. Earthquake detectors are occasionally mentioned in later oriental manuscripts, but in the West the idea of detecting or measuring earthquakes came centuries later, stimulated in part by the catastrophe in Lisbon in 1755 (p 34). Yet another hundred years elapsed before, in 1856, Luigi Palmieri installed in the observatory at Vesuvius a seismograph which was capable of recording the passage of seismic waves, giving their amplitude, time of onset and the direction of the earthquake from the instrument. Reliable instrumental records are generally regarded as starting around the beginning of this century.

A *seismometer* is an instrument to sense earth motion; a *seismograph* combines a seismometer with recording equipment which provides a permanent continuous record of the motion, and the record itself is called a *seismogram*. Typically the sensing device comprises a freely-suspended mass which remains stationary while the supporting mechanism and ground beneath move in earthquake tremors, the mass being damped to prevent oscillations after the tremors have ceased. Many different types of instrument are in operation around the world, some early ones with a mass of many thousands of kilograms, requiring a huge vault to house them. The seismogram is recorded either by a pen on paper, or by a light signal on photosensitive paper, on a rotating drum which acts as a chronograph, accurately recording time. Some instruments of this type are still quite bulky and have to be placed in specially designed vaults located in a remote place so that 'earthquake noise' is not drowned

24 Inside the WWSSN observatory at Eskdalemuir, Scotland

25 A modern model of Zhang Heng's apparatus for detecting earthquakes . . .

S wave

surface waves

by passing traffic and other 'cultural noise'. Modern seismographs tend towards miniaturization, and their signals may be radioed to distant observatories and recorded on magnetic tape.

Today seismic observatories are well distributed over the world, and fig 27 shows the location of stations in the *Worldwide Standardized Seismograph Network* (WWSSN) as well as other stations from which seismogram readings are readily obtainable. Giant strides have been made in seismology following the establishment of the WWSSN in the early 1960s. For the first time, standard equipment with accurately synchronised time-keeping was installed with something approaching global coverage. The WWSSN observatories (fig 24) each contain two sets of three seismometers, placed mutually at right angles, to receive both short- and long-period waves. Whilst WWSSN and other seismographs will pick up seismic signals generated by nuclear explosions, special arrays of seismographs in geometric layouts are used to monitor them accurately. These arrays, together with WWSSN, were set up not only to promote seismological research but also to indentify nuclear explosions, because when test-ban talks started in 1958 existing seismographic coverage was inadequate.

Seismograms are read to provide the information needed to determine epicentre, magnitude and depth of focus. A wealth of other information may also be deduced about the earthquake (pp 20–21) and the rocks through which the seismic waves have travelled (pp 26–27). To fix the epicentre, readings from at least 3 observatories are needed. P waves (p 20) travel faster than S waves, so the time interval which elapses between the arrival of the P wave and the S wave increases with distance from the epicentre. Thus the time interval of 11 minutes in the example at the top of the page, when read off a time-distance graph (of travel-time curves), gives a distance of 90°, a quarter way round the globe. Some seismographs have very high magnification in order to detect earthquakes on the other side of the globe; such instruments are designed to avoid being damaged by large, nearby earthquakes. Other seismographs are triggered to record by the onset of motion; this eliminates the expense of blank record, but the commencement of the wave-train from which epicentre is calculated may be missed. A network of instruments to record very-long-period waves was set up in the late 1970s, as little was known about waves with periods of half an hour to an hour.

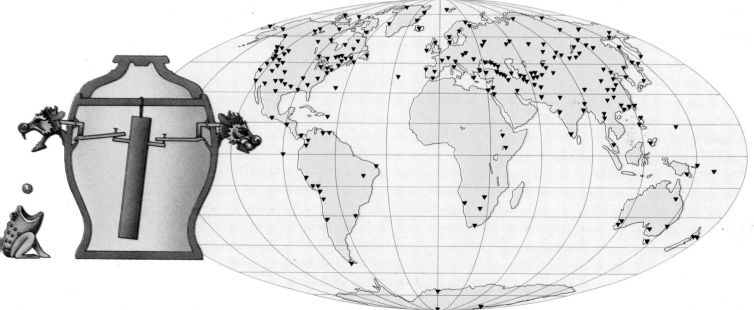

26 . . . and its mode of operation   **27 Distribution of the WWSSN and comparable observatories**

The scales of earthquakes

It has proved difficult to find an adequate way of measuring the size of earthquakes, but two concepts commonly used are *intensity* and *magnitude*. *Intensity* classifies the degree of shaking; it is gauged from inspection of the damage and other effects of an earthquake, and usually is greatest close to the epicentre, diminishing with distance. *Magnitude* is an attempt to compare earthquakes in terms of their total energy or power, and is obtained by measuring the maximum displacement or amplitude of seismogram traces. After a correction has been made for the distance between the focus of the earthquake and the seismograph, magnitude is calculated. Theoretically, calculations of magnitude from various seismic stations should give the same value for the same earthquake.

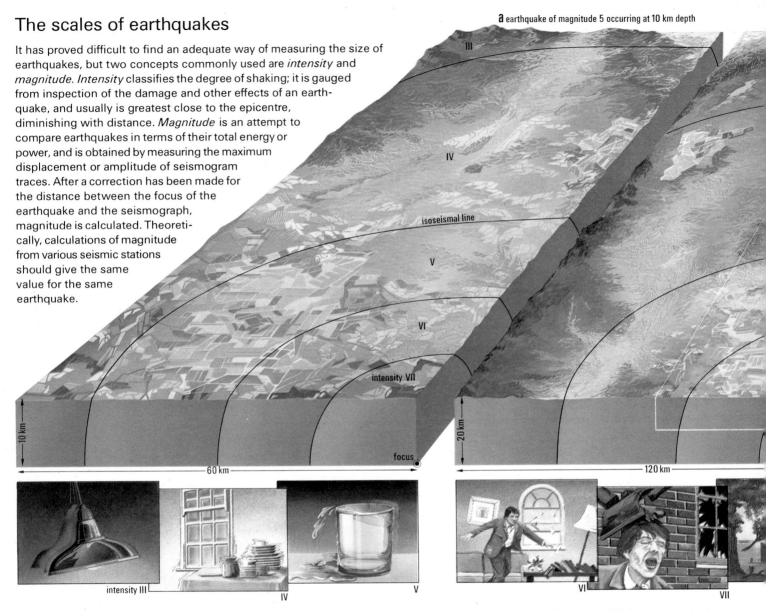

a earthquake of magnitude 5 occurring at 10 km depth

isoseismal line

intensity VII

focus

intensity III

IV

V

VI

VII

Extracts from the Modified Mercalli Intensity Scale
I Not felt. **II** Felt by persons at rest. **III** Felt indoors; hanging objects swing; vibration like passing of light trucks; duration estimated. **IV** Vibration like passing of heavy trucks; windows, dishes, doors rattle. **V** Felt outdoors; sleepers wakened; liquids disturbed, some spilled; doors swing, close, open. **VI** Felt by all; many frightened and run outdoors; windows, dishes, glassware broken; weak plaster and masonry cracked; furniture moved or overturned. **VII** Difficult to stand; hanging objects quiver; fall of plaster, loose bricks, stones, tiles and architectural ornaments; waves on ponds. **VIII** Steering of cars affected; fall of stucco and some masonry walls; twisting, fall of chimneys, factory stacks, monuments, elevated tanks; branches broken from trees.

b earthquake of magnitude 7 occurring at 20 km depth

C earthquake of magnitude 8.6 occurring at 40 km depth

VI

VII

VI

VIII

VII

IX

VIII

X

IX

focus

40 km

240 km

focus

VIII

IX

X

XI

Intensity, expressed in Roman numerals, is purely descriptive. An abridged version of the commonly used *Modified Mercalli Intensity Scale,* number I to XII, is shown below. To determine intensities, information is gathered from replies to questionnaires, and from specialists' reports of damage. Ultimately an *isoseismal map* may be drawn with lines separating areas of equal intensity, around the centre of the earthquake. The illustration shows that by mapping intensity values it is possible to estimate the magnitude and depth of focus from the spacing of intensity contour lines and the maximum intensity value. But in detail the relationship between shaking and magnitude involves many factors.

Magnitude is a concept initially developed by C. F. Richter for comparing sizes of Californian earthquakes. To cover the huge size range of earthquakes, the magnitude scale is logarithmic, each unit representing a tenfold increase in amplitude of the measured waves, and nearly a 30-fold increase in energy. Magnitude can be calculated from P, S, or surface waves, but this gives rise to different magnitudes for the same event. Other discrepancies in magnitudes quoted in news and scientific journals result from the different pathways of the various waves picked up from an individual earthquake. Earthquake waves are produced in a range of frequencies, the highest of which is at the low range of audibility, about 10 Hertz (cycles per second). The lowest frequency may be less than one cycle per hour, and is probably related to the total length of fault slippage. It thus may have a wavelength of 1000 km or more. In very large earthquakes, the proportion of low-frequency waves, and their amplitude, may both be great, but since these waves are beyond the frequency range of most seismographs, they are not used in magnitude calculations. Thus magnitudes over 8 are minima. Duration of shaking is not accounted for in the magnitude concept.

IX General panic; frame structures, if not bolted, shifted off foundations; underground pipes broken; conspicuous cracks in ground; in alluviated areas sand and mud ejected, earthquake fountains, sand craters. **X** Most masonry and frame structures destroyed, some well-built wooden structures and bridges destroyed; serious damage to dams and embankments, large landslides. **XI** Rails bent greatly; underground pipelines completely out of service. **XII** Damage nearly total; lines of sight and level distorted; objects thrown into the air.

Mechanism of earthquakes

Rupture of rocks is the mechanism by which earthquakes are generated. Rock is elastic and can, up to a point, accumulate strain where adjacent areas of rock are subjected to forces pushing or pulling them (fig 29a). It is thought that cracks develop in the rocks as this happens (b). When the stress exceeds the strength of the rock, the rock breaks (c) along a pre-existing or new fracture plane called a *fault*. During rupture, the rocks on either side of the fault-plane move past each other as they jump back (rebound), and the strain is removed. Seismic energy is generated in a train of waves as the rupture extends outwards from its point of origin, the *focus* or *hypocentre*. During rupture, the rock in the quadrants marked 'area of push' (d) pushes or compresses adjacent rock in the direction of motion, and seismographs situated in these quadrants will all receive 'push' as the first direction of movement on the seismogram. Seismographs in the other two quadrants receive 'pull' as the first direction of movement. From analysis of the distribution of 'pushes' and 'pulls', two possible fault planes are inferred, represented by the two white lines in the diagram. One of these planes can be eliminated by examining the orientation of faulting, if visible, in the epicentral region. But care is needed. Fig 31 shows part of the fault trace, 23 km long, produced in a magnitude-7 earthquake: a casual glance at fig 31 suggests that vertical movement has taken place. This is so, but the greater displacement in the earthquake was lateral. If one looks across a lateral fault, and the other side appears to have moved to the right, the fault is said to be *right-lateral*, and if to the left, *left-lateral*. Vertical movement on a fault plane which gives rise to extension is called *normal* faulting; and movement giving rise to compression is *reverse* faulting (fig 30). Gently inclined reverse faults are called *thrusts*.

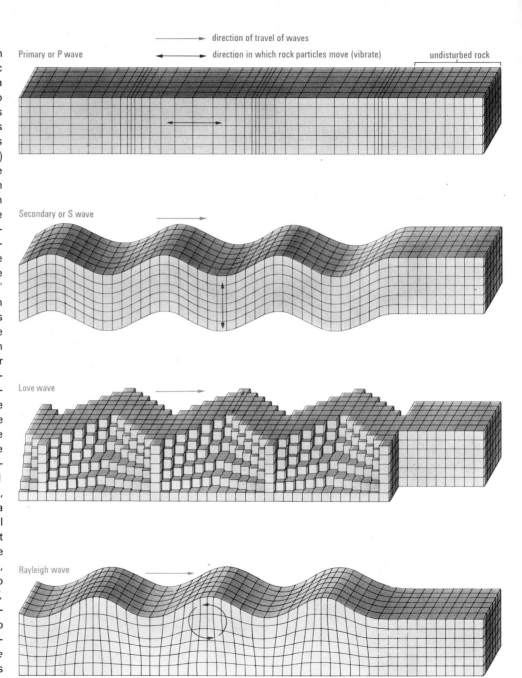

direction of travel of waves
direction in which rock particles move (vibrate)

Primary or P wave
undisturbed rock

Secondary or S wave

Love wave

Rayleigh wave

28 The ways in which earthquake waves travel, distorting the rocks they pass through

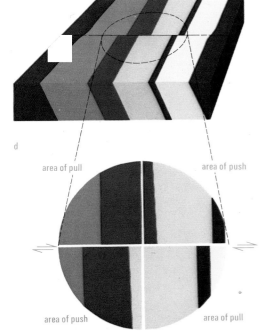

area of pull   area of push

area of push   area of pull

29 The mechanism of earthquakes

Sometimes, for reasons that are not understood, seismic energy is released slowly, taking minutes, days or years; no earthquake is generated, and the rocks slide past each other in a process known as *aseismic slip* or *creep* (p 30–31). At other times, the energy is released violently over a period of seconds as the rock ruptures, producing an earthquake. The seismic energy is emitted from the rupture in three main types of waves. The fastest are the primary or *P waves,* which are compression-dilation waves (fig 28) and travel in average crustal rocks at about 5 kilometres per second. The slower, secondary or *S waves* are shear waves with a speed in the crust of about 3 kilometres per second. Shear waves cannot pass through a liquid and do not penetrate the Earth's outer core (p 26). The slowest waves are *surface waves,* comprising principally *Rayleigh* and *Love waves,* whose depths of penetration are dependent on their wavelengths. Surface waves transmit the bulk of the energy in shallow earthquakes, so that often it is their amplitude which is used to determine magnitude (p 19). In the Chilean earthquake of 1960, surface waves were so powerful they were still being recorded on seismograms 60 hours after the event, having gone round the earth 20 times.

The various types of seismic wave are not radiated equally in all directions and further information on the orientation of the fault plane may be deduced from the wave radiation pattern. The spectrum of waves emitted and their interference patterns give information on the length and mechanism of rupture. Length is confirmed by plotting the foci of aftershocks on the assumption that they occur on the rupture plane of the main event. In this way the orientation and direction of movement – the *focal mechanism* – of the earthquake is deduced for use in regional tectonic studies (p 22–26), risk assessment and earthquake prediction, but this is a lengthy procedure, and may take months, or even years.

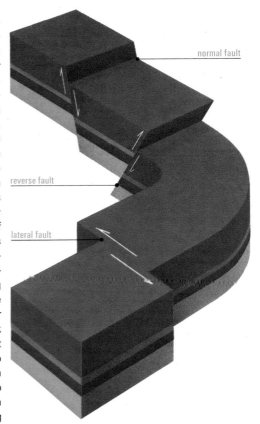

normal fault

reverse fault

lateral fault

30 Types of fault

31 Fault scarp caused by an earthquake, Iran

Plate tectonics

It has long been recognised that earthquakes are not evenly distributed over the Earth. The eventual correlation of this earthquake pattern with the Earth's major surface features, below the oceans as well as on land, was a fundamental key to the evolution of the plate tectonics concept which revolutionised Earth science in the 1970s. The concept is set out in a companion booklet, *The story of the Earth.* The pattern of earthquake distribution and associated surface features was found to define active zones around the Earth. Up to the 1960s seismology alone provided no evidence about the processes at work in these zones. After the establishment of the World-wide Standardized Seismograph Network (p 16), it became possible not only to locate earthquake foci more accurately, but also to determine the focal mechanism of an earthquake — that is to say, which way the rocks moved relative to each other. Determination of earthquake focal mechanisms provided the first independent evidence to confirm that plates move across the surface of the globe, as had already been inferred from other lines of evidence, and to demonstrate direction of movement. Seismology also established the thicknesses of the plates. It showed that the base of the Earth's crust, the Mohorovičić discontinuity (p 27), whilst a fundamental boundary inside the Earth, is not, as might have been thought, the base of the plates. The plates are slabs of *lithosphere* comprising crust *plus* a layer of mantle. The average thickness of oceanic lithosphere is 60 km (of which 6 km is crust), and continental lithosphere 100 km (of which 40 km is crust). Below the lithosphere lies the *asthenosphere,* a zone in which earthquake waves are transmitted more slowly; they are also damped, and the dispersion of surface waves of different wavelengths is increased. The asthenosphere is thus envisaged as a soft layer which is capable of slow movement over long periods of time but in which no earthquakes originate.

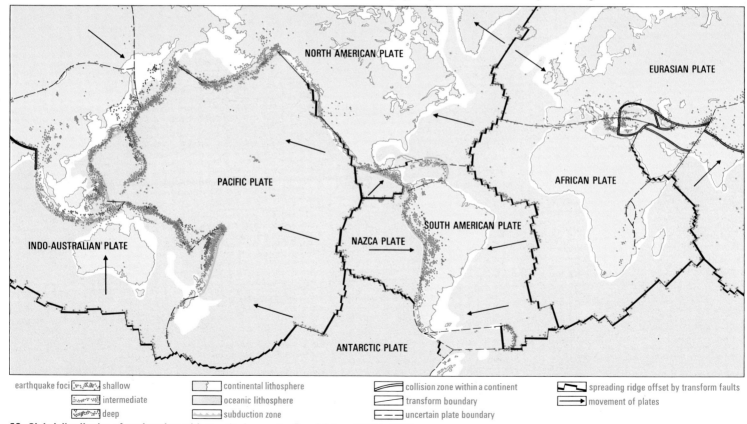

earthquake foci — shallow — intermediate — deep — continental lithosphere — oceanic lithosphere — subduction zone — collision zone within a continent — transform boundary — uncertain plate boundary — spreading ridge offset by transform faults — movement of plates

32 Global distribution of earthquakes with magnitudes greater than 4.5 from 1963 to 1972

Spreading ridges are where new lithosphere is created and two plates are moving apart, and are thus called constructive plate margins. The focal mechanisms of most earthquakes on spreading ridges indicate normal faulting. This implies extension of the lithosphere, confirming that the plates are moving apart (fig 33). These normal faults are parallel with the mountain chain and, where present, the central rift valley, and are fundamental to the origin of these topographic features. Spreading ridges are offset by *transform faults*, which are marked by earthquakes showing lateral movement. But the *direction* of movement revealed in mechanism studies was not as expected. The trans-

form fault in the figure offsets the ridge to the right, but the direction of movement along the active portion of the fault between *a* and *a* is *left*-lateral. Moreover, no earthquakes occur on the so-called *fracture zones* which extend beyond the offset ridge crests (beyond *a* in the figure). These two anomalies revealed the true nature of the transform fault and the spreading mechanism. It is curious that where these inert fracture zones abut continental lithosphere, earthquakes occur. Some earthquakes associated with spreading ridges occur as clusters in time and place and it is thought that these are connected with submarine volcanic eruptions from fissures in the central rift-valley floor.

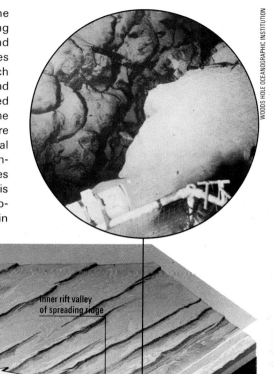

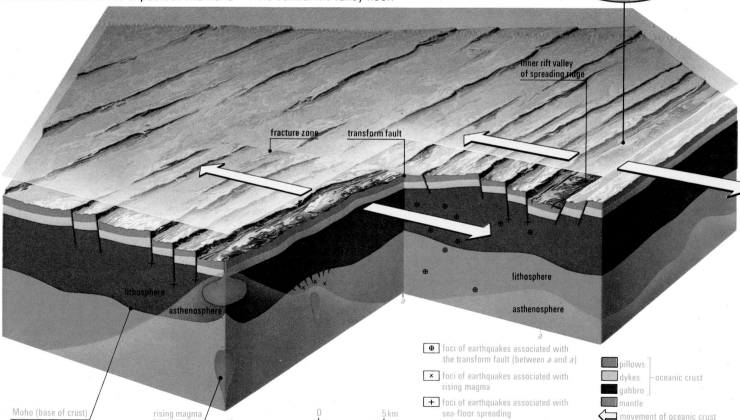

inner rift valley of spreading ridge

fracture zone transform fault

lithosphere

asthenosphere

lithosphere

asthenosphere

Moho (base of crust) rising magma

⊕ foci of earthquakes associated with the transform fault (between *a* and *a*)

× foci of earthquakes associated with rising magma

+ foci of earthquakes associated with sea-floor spreading

pillows
dykes — oceanic crust
gabbro
mantle
⇦ movement of oceanic crust

0   5 km

33 Part of a spreading ridge offset by a transform fault, based on studies in the Atlantic Ocean, and (above) fissure photographed from a submersible craft

Subduction zones are where oceanic lithosphere is consumed as it is drawn down or 'subducted' into the mantle, and are called destructive plate margins. The processes involved are complex and it seems that each subduction zone is different from the next, making generalisations difficult. Earthquake studies have played an important role in the growth of understanding of these plate margins. Initially it was recognised that deep-focus earthquakes were invariably associated with major topographic features as well as with shallower earthquakes (fig 32). Increasingly accurate determination of location and depth of the earthquakes showed them to lie on inclined planes dipping into the mantle to as much as 700 km; these planes were named *Benioff zones*. Because of variations in the speed and amplitude of seismic waves within and around Benioff zones it is inferred that a slab of oceanic lithosphere coincides with each Benioff zone. The more accurate location of earthquake foci afforded by the WWSSN (p16) has revealed much variation in the steepness and continuity of subduction zones; there is therefore no single typical subduction zone. Less is known about the deeper levels of subduction zones because of the relative infrequency of deeper earthquakes.

One of the most intensively studied subduction zones passes underneath Japan. Here the Benioff zone slopes at an angle of 40–45° towards mainland Asia, and earthquakes are distributed all the way down the zone to a depth of 600 km (fig 34); the zone is interpreted as being an unbroken slab of descending lithosphere. Shallow earthquakes in the downgoing slab are associated with fracturing in the outer part of the down-bend in the 100-km-thick lithosphere, or alternatively with thrusting (p20–21). Shallow earthquakes in the overriding slab unexpectedly show tensional rather than compressional movements, implying block uplift and subsidence. Intermediate and deep earthquakes occurring in the cool interior of the descending lithosphere are related to compression or extension

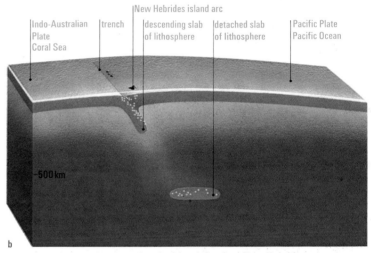

b

35 Foci of earthquakes associated with subduction, New Hebrides

within the slab itself. It has been questioned whether at the pressures prevailing at depths of between 300 and 700 km it is possible for lithosphere to fracture, but even if these deep earthquakes do not represent simple fracturing, it has been shown that their radiation patterns are consistent with the release of shear energy.

The subduction zone beneath the New Hebrides (fig 35) is considerably different from the Japanese zone. Seismic activity shows the lithosphere descending at an angle of 65–70° to a depth of 300 km, with deep earthquakes at 600–650 km; no earthquakes have been observed to originate at depths between 300 and 600 km. Whilst this could be due to the short time over which adequate records have been collected, and the infrequency of activity at this depth, the earthquake-free zone is currently interpreted as a break in the descending lithosphere slab, the detached portion lying horizontally at depth. Many subduction zones have such a break, and it is

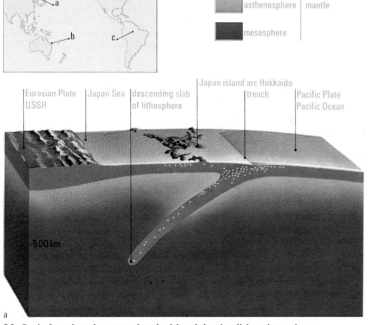

a

34 Foci of earthquakes associated with subducting lithosphere, Japan

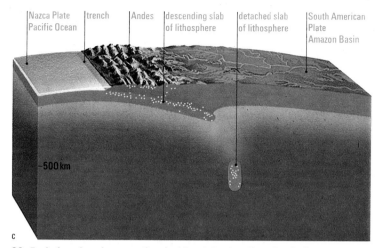

36 Foci of earthquakes associated with subduction, Peruvian Andes

curious that all dip towards the east. Beneath Peru, for example, earthquake distributions show the lithosphere descending at a very gentle angle of 10–15° beneath the continent of South America. Between depths of 200 km and 500 km no earthquakes have been observed. The deep-focus earthquakes below 500 km delineate a detached slab of lithosphere in a vertical attitude (fig 36).

The driving mechanism of plate tectonics is presumed to be some form of circulation within the mantle; the main question is whether the whole mantle is in circulation or only the asthenosphere. There is doubt whether circulation cells could function if restricted to the thin asthenosphere. It is not known whether asthenosphere descends with lithosphere at subduction zones, nor to what depths asthenosphere may continue to exist. Perhaps it will be possible to resolve these questions with velocity and amplitude studies on seismic waves from deep earthquakes, but as yet these methods are only beginning to define the upper and lower limits of the asthenosphere.

Intraplate earthquakes present another problem in plate tectonics. Fig 32 shows a significant number of continental events – some of which were large damaging shocks – not associated with plate boundaries of any sort. Some occur where ocean fracture zones meet continental lithosphere, and may represent old weaknesses which existed in the continental lithosphere prior to the opening of the adjacent ocean. Others within continents are located in geologically older weaknesses which are adjacent and more or less parallel to the continental margins. Still others, for example in central China, originate from old internal weaknesses reactivated by continental collisions such as that of India and Asia.

The San Andreas Fault in California and the Alpine Fault in New Zealand are plate boundaries within continental lithosphere where lateral movement is taking place. They are called transform plate boundaries even though originally the term 'transform' was introduced for those special lateral faults which offset spreading ridges, depicted in fig 33. Recent lateral movement is easily spotted where natural or man-made features are displaced (fig 38). In continental lithosphere the line of the plate boundary is not consistently parallel to the direction of movement between the plates (fig 37), and this geometric relationship seems to control the frequency and magnitude of earthquakes. On the San Andreas system, the great but infrequent earthquakes, such as San Francisco 1906, involve an oblique part of the master fault, while more frequent but nevertheless large earthquakes characterise sections of the fault complex which are parallel to the movement direction. Where the plate boundary is oblique to the plate movement, vertical as well as sideways movement takes place, resulting in reverse faulting and consequent thickening of the lithosphere, demonstrated in the mountains of the Transverse Ranges. Focal mechanisms of earthquakes in this region confirm the reverse faulting which must accompany such compression. On the New Zealand Alpine Fault over 400 km of lateral and 20 km of vertical displacement have resulted in uplift of the Southern Alps (fig 67).

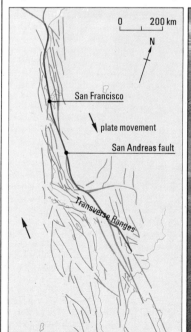

37 The San Andreas Fault system

38 The fault crossing Carrizo Plain

The inside of the Earth

Knowledge of the Earth's interior is pieced together from the way in which seismic waves travel through it: the waves are modified by the density variations and elastic properties of Earth material along their pathways. Interpreting seismograms is highly complex: initially both the source of the seismic waves (the earthquake) and the nature of the transmission medium (the Earth's interior) were unknown. Over the years seismologists have made assumptions about the Earth's interior, and by testing these assumptions against seismograms, little by little our view has become more detailed. Today's picture of the Earth's interior is summarised in fig 39. It was R. D. Oldham who in 1906 first suggested the Earth has a core, and in 1913 Beno Gutenberg calculated the depth of the core-mantle boundary from the sudden decrease in P-wave velocity at 2900 km. Confirmation of this boundary, the *Gutenberg discontinuity*, comes from reflections such as pathway e in fig 39. Pathways like *d* which graze the core show that while this discontinuity is sharp enough to cause the reflection of *c*, it is in some respects transitional because some P and S waves are bent into the shadow zone. Inge Lehmann suggested in 1936 that the core has a solid inner core, on the basis of travel times of waves passing through it. This discovery was confirmed in 1970 when seismographs had become sensitive enough to detect reflections from the boundary. It is clear that there is a low-velocity zone, the *asthenosphere,* in the upper part of the mantle. But low-velocity zones give no reflections and tend to absorb the seismic wave energy rather than transmitting it, so they are not clearly 'seen'. Thus, although it is known that the depth of the upper boundary of the asthenosphere is variable — shallow at spreading ridges (p 23) and deepening in continental regions to 100–150 km — its lower boundary is virtually unknown.

The mantle. Travel times for pathways such as a, b and c indicate that seismic waves travel faster the deeper they penetrate the mantle

The core. P waves travel considerably more slowly in the core than in the mantle, and S waves are not transmitted at all. This indicates that at least the outer part of the core is liquid.

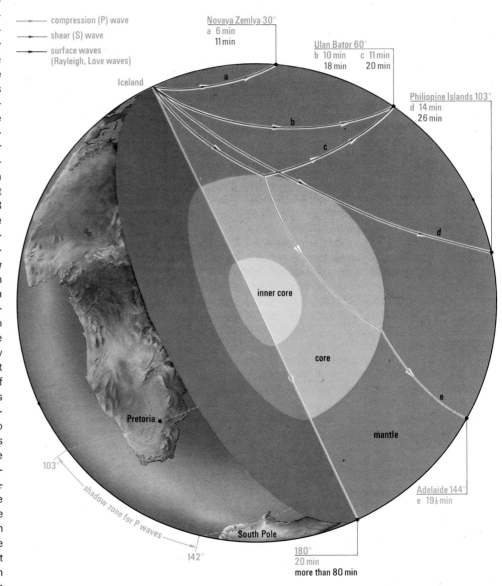

compression (P) wave

shear (S) wave

surface waves (Rayleigh, Love waves)

Iceland

Novaya Zemlya 30°
a 6 min
11 min

Ulan Bator 60°
b 10 min   c 11 min
18 min   20 min

Philippine Islands 103°
d 14 min
26 min

inner core

core

Pretoria

mantle

103°

shadow zone for P waves

South Pole

Adelaide 144°
e 19½ min

142°

180°
20 min
more than 80 min

39 Paths of selected waves through the earth and their travel times, and shadow zone cast by the core

The structure of the Earth's crust can likewise be deduced from analysis of transmitted seismic waves. In 1909 Andrija Mohorovičić, a Croatian seismologist working on travel times of waves from an earthquake near Zagreb, concluded that at a depth of about 50 km there is a discontinuity below which seismic waves travel more rapidly. Now known as the *Mohorovičić* or *M-discontinuity* or, more commonly, the *Moho*, this boundary divides the *crust* from the *mantle*, and is thought to represent a change in composition of Earth material. The depth of the Moho is now known to be highly variable, in general shallow (6 km) under oceans, deeper (40 km) under continents and deepest (60 km) under some young mountain ranges. Within the crust, the travel patterns of artificially-produced seismic waves are used to determine structure. This is one of the principal methods of geophysical prospecting for petroleum and other mineral resources. The depth examined depends on the type and strength of the energy source and the distribution of seismographs, and extends to the full thickness of the crust. The artificial seismic sources may be vibrators which can be tuned to emit a limited spectrum of frequencies, or explosions. A distinct advantage of using artificial seismic sources is that their time and place of origin and source characteristics are known, whereas with natural earthquakes these must be calculated. A 20-year-long study in the European Alps using explosions and also commercial quarry blasts has yielded the analysis in fig 40. It revealed that the Moho, instead of being a sharp discontinuity, is here a transition zone of variable thickness whose greatest depth is 60 km. Furthermore, high-density rocks (lower crustal layers in the figure) are present abnormally near the surface in the core of the Alps. These high-density rocks overlie upper crustal rocks which transmit seismic waves more slowly than expected, and which are interpreted as being partially melted.

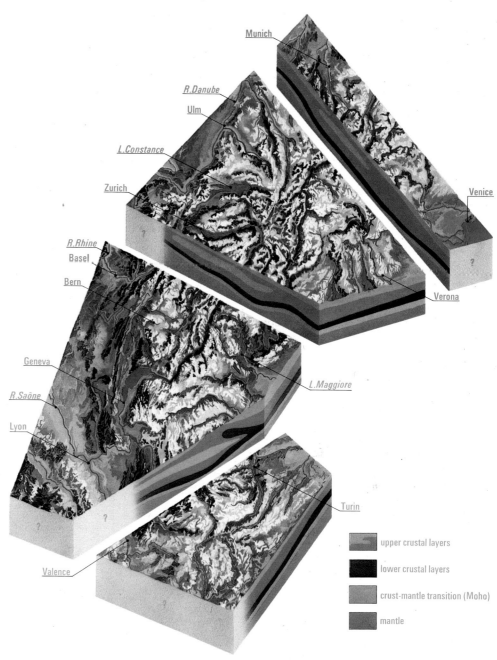

upper crustal layers

lower crustal layers

crust-mantle transition (Moho)

mantle

40 Crustal structure and the Moho beneath the Alps, deduced from explosion seismology

Geological effects of earthquake shaking

A rock and snow avalanche was dislodged from the overhanging, unstable northern face of the Peruvian mountain Nevados Huascarán in 1970 by an offshore earthquake of magnitude 7.7. Eye-witnesses said the avalanche, accompanied by an 'explosion' or 'sonic boom' began during the earthquake shaking. It fell 4000 metres into the Rio Santo valley, preceded by a strong blast of air, and became a turbulent flow of mud and boulders with an average speed of 280 kilometres per hour, shaking the ground as it passed. Boulders became airborne, their impact craters suggesting velocities of 1000 km/hour. The town of Yungay was annihilated, buried under rock debris 10 metres deep, and probably 18 000 people died in this densely populated valley.

41 Nevados Huascarán viewed from Yungay before and after the 1970 avalanche

Submarine avalanches triggered by earthquakes generate *turbidity currents,* great masses of watery sediment which race down the continental slope and come to rest in the ocean deep. The mechanism and magnitude of these currents was not appreciated until 1952 when the timing of a series of breaks in telephone cables, following a 7.2-magnitude earthquake off Newfoundland in 1929 (fig 42), was interpreted as a time-sequence giving the velocity of the turbidity current as it broke through successively distant cables. This interpretation allowed geologists to understand more about submarine erosion and sedimentation, while at the same time explaining an important cause of submarine cable breaks to engineers.

A landslide dammed up water to form a lake in Madison Canyon, Montana, USA, after a 7.1-magnitude earthquake in 1959 (fig 44). The treeless mountainside (centre) is the area from which the slide fell, engulfing a campsite and killing 19 people. In order to eliminate the flood hazard to inhabitants downstream created by damage to the Hebgen Dam further upstream, heavy earthmoving machinery was used to create a spillway through the slide material. Only then could both lakes be drained and repairs made to the Hebgen Dam. Intervals between geyser eruptions at nearby Yellowstone Park were altered, and there were ground level changes with a maximum drop of 6 metres.

Ground level changes are most easily seen at coastlines: the spruce trees in fig 45 were killed by immersion of their roots in sea water, following subsidence of 1 metre caused by the 1964 Alaska earthquake.

Cracks (fig 46) and **local tilting** of the ground surface (p5–7) may be caused by settling and lurching of unconsolidated soft sediments. Whilst such cracks may on occasion be the surface expression of a buried fault, they are usually unrelated to the fault that caused the earthquake.

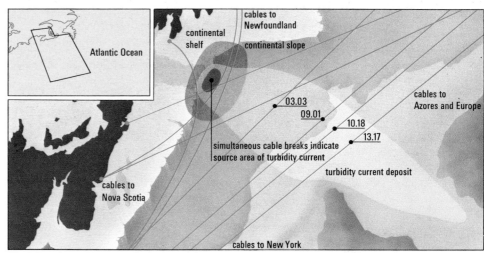

42 Submarine cable breaks in the hours after the Grand Banks earthquake, 1929

43 Earthquake-triggered avalanche in Peru, 1970

45 Subsided coastline, Kenai Peninsula, Alaska

44 Landslide after 1959 earthquake, Montana

46 Ground fissured in 1968, Khorasan, Iran

Evidence of past earthquake movement

Even the very largest earthquakes produce a maximum displacement or offset of only a few metres. Fig 47 shows the lateral offset of five metres which accompanied the 7.1-magnitude Imperial Valley earthquake of 1940. Fig 48 shows a group of faults in Utah, with small offsets. Over a period of time, the combined effect of many earthquakes along the same fault system produces a much greater displacement, either by repeated movement on one fault or movement on a group of faults. Displacements of tens or hundreds of metres on some branches of the San Andreas fault system are seen to disrupt surface topography, indicating that movement is too frequent and too great for erosion to obliterate the surface evidence. In fig 49 ridges and valleys are offset by right-lateral movement (p 20–21); in fig 50 a stream is offset and a *sag pond* is formed where a surface depression now abuts against higher ground on the other side of the fault. Further back in time, the San Andreas system has produced about 300 km of right-lateral movement in the last 12 million years, as demonstrated by the displacement of distinctive rocks. Elsewhere earthquakes accompany uplift of mountain ranges such as the Karakoram (background) and the New Zealand Alps (p 25, fig 67). The height of the mountains depends on the rate of uplift relative to the rate of erosion. In the New Zealand Alps these are about equal, but in the Karakoram, uplift has consistently gained over erosion. Tectonic movement is not always accompanied by earthquakes, as parts of some faults today move extremely slowly, a few centimetres a year (fig 51), by a process known as *aseismic slip* or *creep* (probably promoted by slippery rocks along the fault plane), which does not generate earthquakes. Nevertheless, it is assumed that earthquakes have normally been an accompaniment of tectonic processes in the geological past.

47 Offset of orange trees, California

48 Faults in sandstone, Utah

49 Offset disrupts surface topography, California

50 Pond created by faulting, California

51 Creep disrupts a footpath, California

Earthquake prediction

Today it is taken for granted that weather can be forecast. It seems possible that earthquakes too may one day be predicted with some degree of certainty. The search for reliable earthquake precursors has attracted intense effort (fig 54) in many countries, but no coherent patterns have yet emerged and achievements in earthquake prediction remain very limited. Many of the phenomena considered to be earthquake precursors relate to *dilatancy*, the swelling of rock caused by the development of cracks in response to increasing stress (fig 29b). Other precursors, probably unrelated to dilatancy, include foreshocks, creep and unusual animal behaviour. It is not known whether the whole range of precursors invariably precedes an earthquake; more evidence is needed. The essential first step in all earthquake prediction studies is to identify a region in which the seismic history suggests that an earthquake may be expected to occur soon, so that instrumentation may beneficially be deployed (fig 52). There have been some notable earthquake prediction successes in China, where incentive is high because of a long history of disastrous shocks, and where huge resources of manpower, both amateur and professional, have been devoted to this work. Prior to the Haicheng earthquake of 1975, a north-easterly moving locus of seismicity was spotted following an earthquake in the Bo Hai region

in 1969 and earlier events (fig 52). Fieldwork to determine ground deformation and other precursors led in June 1974 to a specification of the expected event: an earthquake of magnitude 5 to 6 in the northern Bo Hai region within one to two years. In February 1975 a series of small tremors was correctly identified as a foreshock sequence; this triggered the decision to evacuate people to temporary outdoor shelters despite bitter winter weather. Later that day more than a million people were camping out and in the early evening the main shock of magnitude 7.3 and focal depth 12 km occurred. Tragically, the Tangshan (fig 52) earthquake of the following year, in which 240 000 died, was not predicted, in part owing to the apparent absence of foreshocks and other key precursors. Strong shaking was felt in Beijing (Peking) and residents moved to temporary shelter during the aftershock period (fig 53). Western industrialised societies will require high-certainty earthquake prediction before considering obligatory population evacuation as the best means of averting disaster, for false alarms will not easily be tolerated. In California and other sophisticated, populous regions where effort is devoted to earthquake prediction research, the situation is ironic: further increase of knowledge which could enable reliable prediction awaits the occurrence of large earthquakes.

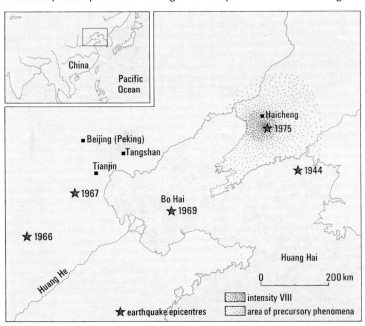

52 The extent of premonitory effects and earthquake damage, Haicheng

53 Camping out in Beijing during the aftershocks of the Tangshan quake

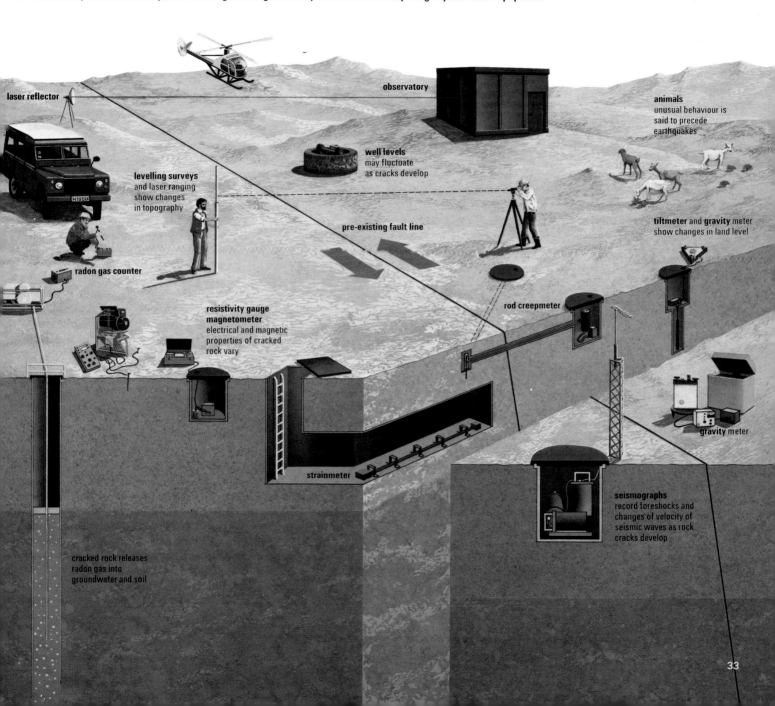

laser reflector

observatory

animals
unusual behaviour is
said to precede
earthquakes

well levels
may fluctuate
as cracks develop

levelling surveys
and laser ranging
show changes
in topography

tiltmeter and **gravity** meter
show changes in land level

pre-existing fault line

radon gas counter

rod creepmeter

**resistivity gauge
magnetometer**
electrical and magnetic
properties of cracked
rock vary

gravity meter

strainmeter

seismographs
record foreshocks and
changes of velocity of
seismic waves as rock
cracks develop

cracked rock releases
radon gas into
groundwater and soil

Famous earthquakes

The Lisbon earthquake of 1755 at half past nine in the morning, lasted ten minutes and had a magnitude of 8¾. In North Africa damage was so intense it was thought there had been a separate earthquake. Tsunamis devastated the waterfront (fig 56). Tens of thousands died in collapsing buildings, and fire broke out, gutting much of the city. Lisbon was a wealthy mercantile city and losses in jewellery, art treasures, books and merchandise were immense, in addition to the loss of life. Europe was stunned. There followed great speculation on the cause of earthquakes: divine punishment, contraction of the earth and electricity were invoked.

The Naples earthquake of 1857, in which perhaps 12000 people died, caused intense damage. The engineer, Robert Mallet, set out to investigate the earthquake effects. His systematic and painstaking methods of observation and measurement were quite novel; from them he inferred that the earthquake was propagated from a point by waves. The magnitude of the earthquake was probably about 6½, but the degree of devastation suggested a much larger event. Mallet attributed the severity of damage to the inadequacy of local building techniques, a point underlined by the damage caused by subsequent earthquakes.

The Assam earthquake of 1897 with a magnitude of 8.7 is one of the largest recorded. Effects in the epicentral region were used to establish intensity XII on the Modified Mercalli Scale. Investigating, R.D. Oldham found evidence that stones 30cm across were flung upwards into the air (fig 60) and he speculated on how heavy stone monuments had rotated on their plinths. This earthquake, occurring at the dawn of the era of instrumental seismology, confirmed that three types of waves are generated (surface waves had been recorded only once before) and that earthquake waves travel faster the deeper they penetrate the Earth.

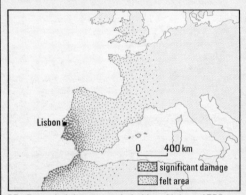

55 Recorded damage and shaking, Lisbon, 1755

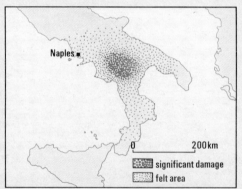

57 Recorded damage and shaking, Italy, 1857

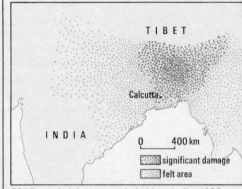

59 Recorded damage and shaking, India, 1897

56 Earthquake effects in Lisbon, 1755

58 Damage near the epicentre at Polla, Italy

60 Stones dislodged by vertical throw, India, 1897

The San Francisco earthquake of 1906 shook all California: occurring just after 5 am, the shaking wakened people, throwing some from their beds. The epicentre was near the Golden Gate, so San Francisco was severely hit, with intensity XII in some areas. Movement along more than 400 km of the San Andreas fault, with an average offset of 4 metres, resulted in an earthquake of 8.3 magnitude, severe shaking probably lasting less than a minute. The ground was seen to undulate; there were sand fountains in valleys, landslides in hilly ground, large trees broken and thrown to the ground, monuments and statues displaced or upended; cattle and horses were unable to stand, and aftershocks persisted for a year. Fires broke out in San Francisco (fig 62), and fire fighting was impeded because water supply lines were broken in poor ground and where they crossed the fault. As many houses were built of timber the ensuing 3-day conflagration caused huge losses. Damage to drains caused

sanitary problems (above). The official report showed that high intensities corresponded with the fault line and with valleys containing soft sediments (fig 61). In the city there was a clear difference in degree of damage between those structures built on made ground (intensity X) and those on adjacent bedrock (intensity VII). The report also commented that damage was related to building style and fabric; wooden buildings survived the shaking much better than those built of brick or stone. In considering the cause of the earthquake, H. F. Reid put forward a theory of the mechanism of rock rupture (see p 21) known as the *elastic rebound theory*, and suggested that if strain could be adequately measured, earthquakes could be predicted. From the collected seismograms, he drew up travel-time curves showing the arrival times of seismic waves at observatories at different distances from the epicentre — a standard against which future earthquake epicentres could be located (p16.)

San Francisco

Los Angeles

0   200 km

significant damage
felt area

61 Damage and shaking, California, 1906

62 Fire sweeping through San Francisco in the days following the earthquake and (inset) Damage on made ground

The Great Alaska earthquake of 1964 which occurred at dusk on Good Friday, is one of the largest ever recorded and is exceptionally well documented. Many phenomena associated with it are described in this booklet. The magnitude is often quoted as 8.6, but with such large events the magnitude scale is not very meaningful. The total energy release was probably the equivalent of 60 one-megaton bombs, and double that of the San Francisco 1906 earthquake, which had 8.3 magnitude. Ground shaking was severe and prolonged, lasting perhaps 7 minutes altogether with 3 minutes of damaging intensity. Although damage was confined to a tenth of Alaska (fig 66), in 1964 this area comprised the economic heart-land of the state containing half of the population. The death toll was low, 115 in Alaska, of whom most were presumed killed by the devastating water waves. Fortunately the earthquake did not coincide with high tide or the fishing season, when the death toll would have been much higher. Few people were injured by collapsing buildings as most buildings were of earthquake-resistant construction. Also, since it was a holiday, commercial buildings were closed. Failure of the ground by liquefaction (fig 63) and consequent landsliding caused much damage to property, whilst some damage was attributable to poor workmanship. At Seward, oil storage tanks caught fire (fig 65) and burning oil was spread by the water waves. Ground motion was less severe at Kodiak, which was situated on bedrock, but water waves swept ships inland (fig 64). Huge areas were raised or lowered by about 2 metres, and locally as much as 17 metres. The length of fault which ruptured is estimated to have been between 500 and 1000 km, but evidence of faulting was rarely seen (much was submarine). The mechanism of the earthquake was deduced to be low-angle thrusting of the Pacific oceanic lithosphere under the continental lithosphere to the north. The rupture itself propagated from the epicentre predominantly southwestwards in a series of jerks.

63 Buildings damaged by landsliding, Anchorage

64 Ships swept ashore by water waves, Kodiak

65 Devastated port and rail terminal, Seward

66 Recorded damage and shaking, Alaska, 1964

Further reading: *Earthquakes* by G.Eiby, Heinemann, 1980; *Earthquakes: a primer* by Bruce A. Bolt, Freeman, 1978; *Earthquake Information Bulletin,* a bimonthly periodical for general and specialised readers, can be purchased from Branch of Distribution, Text Products Section, US Geological Survey, 604 South Pickett Street, Arlington, Virginia 22202; *Earthquakes and volcanoes,* Bruce A. Bolt, Freeman, 1980.

The Story of the Earth, a permanent exhibition at the Geological Museum in South Kensington, London, explains the fundamentals of modern earth science. Highlights of the exhibition include an audiovisual presentation about the Alaska earthquake of 1964 with special shaking effects.